Jonathan Edwards

by Simonetta Carr

with Illustrations by Matt Abraxas

REFORMATION HERITAGE BOOKS

Grand Rapids, Michigan

Reformation Heritage Books
2965 Leonard St. NE
Grand Rapids, MI 49525
616-977-0889 / Fax: 616-285-3246
e-mail: orders@heritagebooks.org
website: www.heritagebooks.org

Printed in the United States of America
14 15 16 17 18 19/10 9 8 7 6 5 4 3 2 1

Library of Congress Control Number: 2014947274

For additional Reformed literature, request a free book list from Reformation Heritage Books at the above address.

CHRISTIAN BIOGRAPHIES FOR YOUNG READERS

This series introduces children to important people in the Christian tradition. Parents and schoolteachers alike will welcome the excellent educational value it provides for students, while the quality of the publication and the artwork make each volume a keepsake for generations to come. Furthermore, the books in the series go beyond the simple story of someone's life by teaching young readers the historical and theological relevance of each character.

AVAILABLE VOLUMES OF THE SERIES
John Calvin
Augustine of Hippo
John Owen
Athanasius
Lady Jane Grey
Anselm of Canterbury
John Knox
Jonathan Edwards

SOME ANTICIPATED VOLUMES
Marie Durand
Martin Luther
…and more

Table of Contents

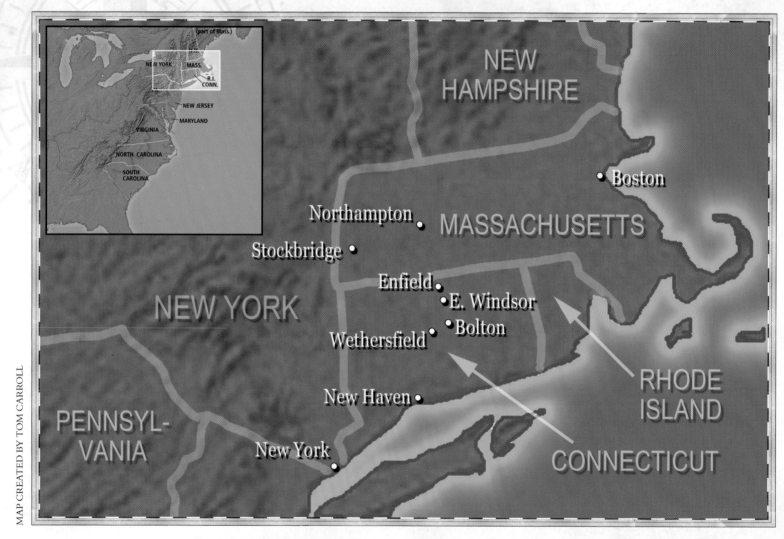

A map of New England during Jonathan Edwards's life. You may want to use it to follow his travels.

Introduction

Many people remember Jonathan Edwards as the preacher of a scary sermon about a spider dangling over a fire. In reality, there was much more than that to his life and thought—so much so that he is considered one of North America's brightest minds. He lived at a time when many people were seriously questioning long-accepted ideas about the world, life, and God. His answers to these questions have left a mark on the way we think today. He is especially remembered for his important role in the eventful time of history called the First Great Awakening.

Jonathan Edwards, portrayed by a later artist (John Ferguson Weir (1841–1926))

CHAPTER ONE

An Inquisitive Child

NANCY HOULIHAN

The Loomis Homestead in Windsor, Connecticut, one of the oldest timber-frame houses in America. The oldest part of the house was built in 1640, so it was standing when Edwards was a child. Edwards's home might have looked similar to this.

Jonathan Edwards was born in East Windsor, Connecticut, a small village next to the Connecticut River, on October 5, 1703. At that time, the United States of America had not yet been formed, and Connecticut was still a British colony ruled by England. Both his father, Timothy, and his maternal grandfather, Solomon Stoddard, were pastors. Jonathan's parents probably hoped their son would become a pastor too, especially because he was the only boy in his family. He had ten sisters, and girls could not become pastors.

Young Jonathan heard his father preach in church and lead family devotions at home. During the day, his parents taught basic school subjects to their son and daughters as well as to some of the town's children. Jonathan's older sisters often helped him review his lessons. Timothy had high expectations for his only son, and Jonathan tried hard not to disappoint him.

Along with school, the family was busy with chores because most modern machines had not been invented. Also, life was filled with dangers. Many diseases were still without a cure, and quite a few children died young. The Edwards family must have been very thankful that all their children grew up healthy.

War was another constant danger. Even though East Windsor was a fairly quiet place, there were battles all around America, mostly between the English and French colonists, each backed by their Native American allies. The family prayed daily for safety for themselves and others, especially in dangerous times. In 1704, they prayed several times a day when relatives who lived in Deerfield, Massachussetts, were captured—and some killed—by a group of French and Native American soldiers from Canada.

FROM DEERFIELD 1704, L'ULTIMO AVAMPOSTO DELLA FRONTIERA. WATERCOLOR ON PAPER BY LELE VIANELLO, COMIC BOOK, TEXT BY CARLO BAZAN AND ILLUSTRATIONS BY LELE VIANELLO, ©LELE VIANELLO AND EDIZIONI SEGNI D'AUTORE, 2014.

An artist's view of the Deerfield raid

THE LANDING OF THE PILGRIMS AT PLYMOUTH, MASS. DEC. 22ND 1620.

An artist's view of the landing of English Pilgrims at Plymouth, Massachusetts, in 1620

Probably Jonathan heard his parents talk about past times when their grandfathers and other Christians had come to America from England to find a place where they could worship according to their convictions. Initially, most of them had hoped to found a new society based on the teachings of the Bible, but, as time passed, some had lost interest in that goal and went to church only because they had to. Like most pastors, Timothy Edwards was concerned and tried to inspire the people in his church to show that their religion must be more than just words.

Jonathan took his father's words to heart. When he was nine, he prayed five times a day, often by himself in the woods. He and his friends also built a shed by an isolated swamp where they could pray and read the Bible together. After a while, however, he found it difficult to keep up with such great efforts. Feeling discouraged, he stopped trying for a while.

Nine-year-old Jonathan Edwards and his friends built a shed by a swamp
where they could pray and read the Bible together.

CHAPTER TWO
Student and Pastor

YALE UNIVERSITY ART GALLERY

Yale College in New Haven, Connecticut, depicted about thirty years after Edwards first moved there

Jonathan was just turning thirteen when he entered a college at Wethersfield, only ten miles from home. He was younger than the average college student, but this was not unusual in those days. Young people could enter college at an early age as long as they could read, write, and understand Latin and Greek. After two years at Wethersfield, Edwards moved to another branch of the school in New Haven, Connecticut. Today, this school is called Yale University.

Edwards didn't make many friends at college. He was a serious young man with little patience for students who spent their free time playing cards or pulling pranks. His personality was quiet, and he was happy just reading and studying. His favorite place in the college was the library, where he read many new, exciting books.

Some books were suggesting new ideas about nature and life. In England, Isaac Newton had just discovered some important laws of nature that related especially to motion, gravity, and light, and he had confirmed and matured theories proposed by scientists before him. In his work, Newton relied heavily on experiments and observation.

Isaac Newton

Edwards was fascinated with Newton's work. In college he wrote papers on rainbows and light, testing Newton's discoveries and trying to answer new questions. He was especially interested in spiders—mostly forest spiders. He wanted to determine how they built their webs and how they could jump from one bush to another as if they were flying or "swimming in the air."

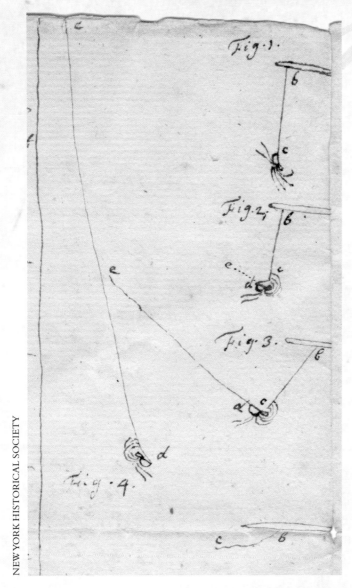

A sketch by Jonathan Edwards describing his experiments with spiders from a letter he wrote to Judge Paul Dudley

Edwards spent a lot of time in observation. Once, he kept a spider on a stick close to his eye and shook the stick until the spider produced a string from its tail. You can read about this experiment in a paper he wrote a few years later known as the "Spider Letter."

As he performed these experiments, he thought about God and His goodness. For example, seeing the spiders having a great time while gliding through the air, he realized that God gives all His creatures not only what they need but also many things that give them joy.

Edwards wanted to discover how spiders built their webs and glided through the air.

Newton's work was particularly important at that time because it made clear that the universe follows some fixed laws. To many people, including Edwards, this showed the greatness of God, who has engineered a wise and careful plan to preserve His creation. To others, this showed instead that because of those laws, God had been able to leave the universe and its people to themselves while He just watched from a distance. Today we call these people *deists*.

Edwards disagreed with the deists. As he had always been taught, he believed God keeps the universe running—even if He uses natural laws to do it—and works directly in all of our lives according to His plan.

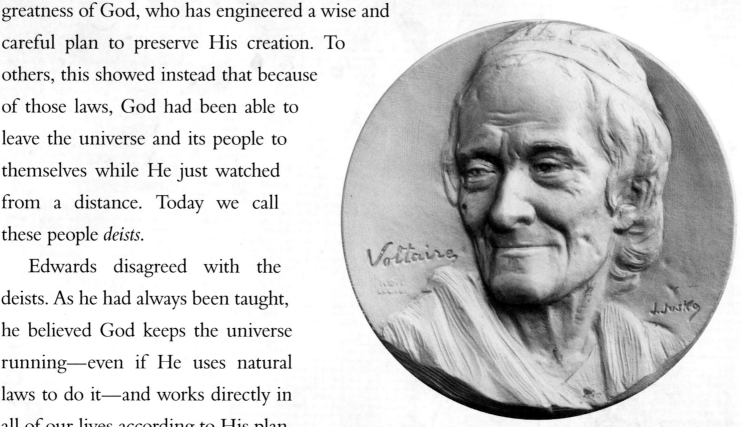

François-Marie Arouet, known as Voltaire, was one of the most influential deists of his time. He thought God was not only distant but also unjust because He let people suffer. Jonathan Edwards answered some of these challenges in books he wrote later in life.

LIBRARY OF CONGRESS

At the same time, some things in the Bible were difficult for Edwards to accept. If God ruled over everything and controlled every event, that means He also controlled who went to heaven and who didn't. At first, Edwards didn't think this was fair. These thoughts made him feel discouraged and worried.

One day, when Edwards was seventeen, one Bible verse, 1 Timothy 1:17, stood out to him more than others: "Now unto the King eternal, immortal, invisible, the only wise God, be honour and glory for ever and ever." He had heard those words many times before, but this time it was different. He felt the Holy Spirit was filling his soul with a new sense of God's glory, wisdom, and justice. He understood God's decisions are all perfect and that it is a great privilege to know Him.

From that time on, everything around him seemed more meaningful. "God's excellency, his wisdom, his purity and love, seemed to appear in everything," he wrote, "in the sun, moon, and stars; in the clouds, and blue sky; in the grass, flowers, trees; in the water, and all nature." Often, Edwards felt so impressed by God's glory and beauty that he started to sing.

He even lost his fear of thunderstorms, which had terrorized him all his life. In those days, people had less protection from lightning, and thunderstorms were more deadly than they are today. After realizing the greatness of God, however, he said he took those opportunities "to view the clouds, and see the lightnings play, and hear the majestic and awful voice of God's thunders, which oftentimes was exceedingly entertaining."

With this daily inspiration, Edwards continued to study for a master's degree at Yale. For some time during his studies, he accepted an invitation to be a substitute pastor in a church in New York City.

With less than ten thousand people, New York was eight hundred times smaller than it is today. At that time, it was still considered a fairly large city. It was an especially busy seaport full of people coming, going, and bringing new ideas. For Edwards, it was more interesting than any other place he had lived. There, he met people from other countries and was exposed to different views.

When Edwards understood the greatness of God, he lost his fear of thunderstorms and enjoyed watching them.

In New York, Edwards continued to take long walks in nature, especially along the banks of the Hudson River. He was often joined by his landlady's son, who was about six years older than he was. The two young men became good friends and enjoyed talking as fellow Christians about the Bible and the future of the church.

At this time Edwards kept an accurate diary, which helps us to understand what he was thinking and how he was feeling. We know he still had many times of discouragement, but he learned to fight them by praying, reading the Bible, and keeping busy. He also wrote a list of seventy resolutions that, by God's grace, he hoped to keep. The first four were all about living for the glory of God. Edwards decided to review this list once a week so he would never forget it.

Resolved, never to do any manner of thing, whether in soul or body, less or more, but what tends to the glory of God; nor be, nor suffer it, if I can avoid it.

Resolved, to live with all my might, while I do live.

Resolved, never to do anything out of revenge.

Resolved, to study the Scriptures so steadily, constantly, and frequently, as that I may find, and plainly perceive myself to grow in the knowledge of the same.

Here are some examples of the resolutions that, by God's grace, Edwards hoped to keep.

In April 1723, his temporary pastorate came to an end, and, with great sadness, Edwards had to say good-bye to his landlady and her family. "My heart seemed to sink within me at leaving the family and city where I had enjoyed so many sweet and pleasant days," he said. "As I sailed away, I kept sight of the city as long as I could." He found comfort by turning his thoughts to heaven, "where these persons that appear so lovely in this world will really be inexpressibly more lovely and full of love to us."

At home, Edwards had to decide what to do next. To obey his father, he accepted a pastoral call in the nearby small town of Bolton, but this was not his first choice. He would have preferred to serve in an exciting place like New York. Wondering if God could use his passion for science, he also finalized some of his scientific writings, hoping they would be published in London. Regardless, he continued to put his heart into his pastorate until the college at Yale called him back to work there as tutor.

A view of New York in Edwards's day. From *A South Prospect of Ye Flourishing City of New York* by John Harris.

A SOUTH PROSPECT OF Yᴱ FLOURISHING **CITY OF NEW-YORK** IN THE PROVINCE OF NEW YORK, NORTH AMERICA.

The job at Yale was more demanding than Edwards had imagined. No one was appointed to lead the college, so the tutors had to take turns filling that position and keeping the unruly students in line. He often felt overwhelmed and discouraged.

Mrs. Jonathan Edwards (Sarah Pierpont Edwards), by Joseph Belcher, c. 1750

In spite of this, he had some reasons to be happy at Yale. First of all, he could find time to retreat in the library he loved. Also, in the city of New Haven was a young lady he admired very much. Her name was Sarah Pierpont, and she was the daughter of one of the founders of Yale.

Edwards had known Sarah's family for some time. From the start he had been struck by her sweet and cheerful spirit and her love for God. "She will sometimes go about from place to place, singing sweetly, and seems to be always full of joy," he wrote. He continued to visit her, and, in 1725, they were engaged to be married.

Sarah Pierpont impressed Edwards with her cheerful spirit and love for God.

DAVID BOYD

The Manse, where Edwards lived with his grandparents after moving to Northampton. As time got closer to his marriage to Sarah, he bought a house with some land where he could start his own family.

Before getting married, Edwards needed a more stable position than college tutor. The answer came from his grandfather, Solomon Stoddard, about a year after his engagement. Stoddard, who had been a pastor in the town of Northampton, Massachusetts, for over sixty years, invited Edwards to be his assistant. It was a great responsibility because Stoddard's church was one of the largest in New England. Edwards felt this call was of God and was installed as assistant pastor on February 15, 1727. About five months later, he married Sarah.

The pastorate kept Edwards busy. He usually woke up at four or five every morning. When he could, he spent up to thirteen hours a day in his study. Even when he rode his horse for 'exercise, he carried along a pen, scraps of paper, and a bottle of ink to write down new ideas. Then he would pin the papers to his coat. At home, Sarah usually helped him take off the papers and organize them in the correct order.

Sarah helped Edwards organize the notes he had pinned to his coat.

CHAPTER THREE
The Great Awakening

dwards's responsibilities increased when Solomon Stoddard died in February 1729. As senior pastor of a church of about thirteen hundred people, he found the workload very difficult for his frail health. Many church members, however, offered their help. They even built him a "good large barn" where he could store the products of his land.

Like all faithful pastors, Edwards was concerned about the people in his church who didn't take God and His Word seriously. Young people were especially carefree and even disrespectful to those in authority. Things changed one day in 1734 when a young man died from a sudden illness. At that point, his friends became worried about their lives. Edwards took this chance to read what the Bible has to say about our short lives on earth and to tell them once again about the love of Christ, who has defeated death forever for those who trust in Him alone for salvation.

This time everyone listened carefully. Soon, not only the young people but many others of all ages and backgrounds became deeply interested in knowing more about God. Besides the regular Sunday services, Edwards set up weekly meetings where people prayed, studied Scripture, and sang songs together. It was a humbling and exciting time. In 1737, in a report called *A Faithful Narrative of the Surprising Work of God*, Edwards expressed his wonder at that "remarkable pouring out of the Spirit of God." "God has seemed to have gone out of His usual way in the quickness of His work," he said. "It is wonderful that persons should be so suddenly and yet so greatly changed."

A renewed interest in God and religion by a large group of people has often been called a *revival* or *awakening*. These events and the rousing times that followed have become known as the First Great Awakening.

Soon, Edwards's report was published in other parts of America and even in England, inspiring other Christians as similar revivals began in many places. One of these Christians was a well-known English preacher named George Whitefield.

DAVID ALEXANDER

A statue of Isaac Watts, a famous hymn writer who lived around Edwards's time. By the time Edwards was a young man, Watts's hymns were already being used in New England in family devotions and other meetings like the ones Edwards set up in Northampton.

George Whitefield, by R. J. Boulton of Cheltenham, nineteenth-century sculptor, Gloucester
PETER CLARKSON

George Whitefield was an unusual preacher. He used large gestures and spoke with such a loud voice that as many as twenty-five thousand people could hear him without a microphone. He also spoke with so much expression that he could move some people by the way he pronounced a simple word like *Mesopotamia*. The best thing about Whitefield, however, is that he preached the gospel—the good news of salvation by grace alone, only through faith in Christ.

In the American colonies, Whitefield was well received, and news was spreading of thousands of people being converted to faith in Christ through his preaching. When Edwards heard that Whitefield was also planning to visit New England, he invited him to Northampton but warned him not to expect too much. Three years had passed since Edwards's report of the revival, and many things had changed. Misunderstanding the message, some people had started to look to themselves and their failures instead of to Christ, and much of the enthusiasm had died down. In spite of this, Whitefield accepted the invitation, and the two preachers met in Northampton on October 17, 1740. At that time, Edwards was thirty-seven and Whitefield, twenty-six.

Edwards and Whitefield were very different. Whitefield was short and stocky while Edwards was tall and thin. Whitefield was impulsive and made decisions quickly while Edwards was particularly careful about everything he did and said. Whitefield used his whole body in preaching and walked around as he spoke without looking at his notes. Edwards kept his body almost still, his voice fairly low, and his face serious as he read most of his carefully written sermons from the pulpit. In spite of their differences, they admired and appreciated each other.

During his short visit, Whitefield preached four times, both at Edwards's church and in other nearby places. He brought almost everyone to tears, including Edwards, who thought the revival was starting again.

Before Whitefield left, Jonathan and Sarah asked him to speak privately to their children. At that time, only seven of their eleven children were born. The oldest, named Sarah after her mother, was twelve years old. The two youngest, Timothy and Susannah (two years old and three months old), were still too small to understand.

Whitefield was impressed by the Edwardses and their children. "A sweeter couple I have not yet seen," he said. He had great admiration for Edwards's wife, Sarah, who had "a meek and quiet spirit [and] talked solidly of the things of God." He was also pleased to see the children wearing simple clothes, unlike many fashionable families at that time.

At the end of Whitefield's stay, Edwards escorted him for two days until they reached East Windsor. There, they visited Edwards's parents, who were about seventy years old at that time. Whitefield said they reminded him of Zechariah and Elizabeth in the Bible.

During the trip, Edwards heard Whitefield preach outdoors to thousands of people who had traveled long distances in spite of the blustery weather. One farmer described the scene by saying, "Every horse seemed to go with all his might to carry his rider to hear the news from heaven for the saving of their souls."

Before Whitefield left, Jonathan and Sarah asked him to speak privately to their children. Probably young Sarah (12), Jerusha (10), Esther (8), Mary (6), and Lucy (4) attended the meeting. Later, Edwards said this talk brought much fruit in the children's lives.

Edwards shared the people's excitement and had great hopes for the revivals, but he also had some disagreements, which he discussed with Whitefield. He especially disagreed when people questioned the faith of pastors who were not as passionate in preaching as Whitefield was. He knew only God could judge the heart. He also feared these comments would drive people away from their churches.

Edwards was also concerned that the people's excitement could get out of hand and draw attention to human feelings instead of what Christ had done for sinners. This became obvious when, nine months later, he preached in the nearby town of Enfield. As in the past, he kept his voice low and avoided big gestures. Still, his sermon, entitled "Sinners in the Hands of an Angry God," was so powerful that his listeners started to cry out, "What shall I do to be saved?" Sadly, however, some of their cries became extreme, and most likely didn't allow Edwards to come to the answer he had prepared: "Christ has flung the door of mercy wide open and stands in the door calling and crying with a loud voice to poor sinners."

Edwards's sermon was so intense that his listeners started to moan and cry aloud.

In this sermon, Edwards wanted to help people understand that sin is a terrible rebellion against God and that anyone who refuses to repent rightly deserves God's punishment. His message was nothing new because his listeners knew very well Jesus' warnings about hell. In fact, he had preached the same sermon in his church without the same extreme reaction.

This matter of excessive emotions and especially the emphasis some people put on them over the quiet, more common work of the Spirit in the local churches started to divide Christians in the American colonies. Those who supported the revivals were called New Lights or, in other cases, New Side, while those who opposed them were called Old Lights or Old Side. Edwards was invited to talk about these problems at Yale. There, he agreed that a display of emotions is not necessarily a sign of true faith. At the same time, he strongly defended the revivals as a great and extraordinary saving work of the Holy Spirit. Later, when some of the excitement had quieted down, he summed up his thoughts in a book called *Religious Affections*. This book became a great classic and has been reprinted many times until today.

CHAPTER FOUR

Sorrow and Rejection

The Besieging of Cape Britton by Land and Sea, a scene from the 1740–1748 French and Indian War (King George's War)

In the meantime, war broke out again in America between the British, on one side, and the French and their Native American allies on the other. This war is called the French and Indian War. Because Northampton was a military headquarters, it was a possible target for attacks. It was a difficult time. "We have been in much fear of an army suddenly rushing in upon the town in the night to destroy it," Edwards wrote. In his sermons, he encouraged the people in the town to pray and remember God's larger plan of eternal salvation.

These attacks, in fact, only increased his desire to bring the gospel of salvation to the Native Americans. He talked about this to his uncle John Stoddard, a wise military man, who was trying to persuade the governor to treat the natives with justice and kindness instead of deceiving them as many British men had been doing.

Native Americans and colonists trading fur for other goods. Trade with the natives was one of the main reasons for the war.

LIBRARY OF CONGRESS

Around this time, David Brainerd, a missionary to the Native Americans, arrived at the Edwards home. For three years, he had risked his life to preach powerfully to the natives what Christ had done to bring them peace with God. When he arrived in Northampton, he was in the last stages of tuberculosis, a deadly illness that made it difficult for him to travel, work, and even breathe. By that time, Sarah was busy with three young children—four-year-old Eunice, two-year-old Jonathan, and newborn Elizabeth—so she asked her seventeen-year-old Jerusha to care for Brainerd's needs.

Jerusha took her nursing job seriously. She even followed Brainerd on a trip during the summer. Some say that Brainerd knew Jerusha before he moved to Northampton and that there was a special love between them, but we don't know for sure.

Jerusha Edwards cared for David Brainerd, who suffered from tuberculosis.

In October, however, Brainerd's health took a turn for the worse. Within days, it was obvious that his life had reached its end. Before dying, Brainerd told Jerusha, "If I thought I should not see you and be happy with you in another world, I could not bear to part with you. But we shall spend a happy eternity together!" He was twenty-nine at that time. Preaching at his funeral, Edwards stressed that when believers die, they are immediately with Christ, where they find eternal joy.

Edwards drew comfort from this same truth when, only four months later, his daughter Jerusha died suddenly of a high fever. She was considered "the flower of the family." Edwards's sorrow was so great that eight months later he confessed in a letter to a friend that he was still aching. In this, he understood God was teaching him "how to sympathize with the afflicted." Edwards buried Jerusha next to Brainerd's grave, where their bodies could await together their resurrection.

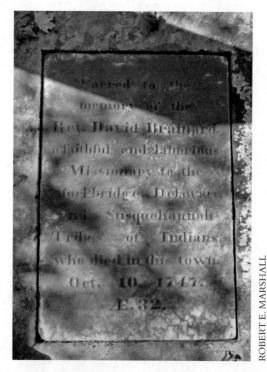

ROBERT E. MARSHALL

David Brainerd's grave

MICAH LARSEN

Jerusha's grave, standing next to Brainerd's

Soon after the deaths of Brainerd and Jerusha, Edwards worked hard to edit and publish the young missionary's diary, pointing out how Brainerd devoted his life to the glory of God and persevered in his job as a missionary even when he couldn't see many results. At a time when, more than ever before, people were turning their attention to personal happiness and rights, the book became a best seller. It has been reprinted dozens of times since then.

In the meantime, Edwards was having some disagreements with the people in his church, especially about the Lord's Supper. Many years earlier, Pastor Solomon Stoddard had started a practice allowing all those who were baptized (nearly everyone was baptized as a baby) and were well behaved to receive the Supper even without professing their faith in Christ as their only Savior. Edwards believed this was wrong. The Bible has a strong warning for those who take the Lord's Supper "unworthily" (1 Cor. 11:27). To Edwards, "unworthily" meant not having true faith and not understanding the meaning of the sacrament.

The people at his church, on the other hand, wanted to keep the old practice. Edwards knew his insistence would cause problems for him and his family, but he finally decided he could not go back on his convictions. This caused a great upset. On June 22, 1750, a large majority of church members (230 of 253) voted that Edwards should leave. On July 2, Edwards preached his farewell sermon to his church, where he had served as pastor for over twenty-three years.

With a large family to support, Edwards thought carefully about his future. He didn't want to stay in Northampton, even if he had some supporters, because he didn't want to divide the town by building a different church. Being well known, he started to receive invitations from other churches in America and even Scotland. The decision was difficult. He wrote to a friend, "I am now as it were thrown upon the wide ocean of the world, and know not what will become of me and my numerous and chargeable family." At that time, the last of his eleven children, Pierpont, was only a few months old.

CHAPTER FIVE
Missionary to the Natives

LEON REED

The Mission House in Stockbridge, built in 1742 on a hillside overlooking the plain. The Edwards family chose to live in a smaller house closer to the natives.

After much thought and prayer, in February 1751 Edwards felt called to accept an invitation to pastor a church in a small village called Stockbridge, about forty miles west of Northampton. Stockbridge was not a usual colonial town. It had been built about fifteen years earlier as a mission to the Native Americans and was composed of about 250 Mohicans, 60 Mohawks, and only a few people of English descent—mostly Edwards's cousins.

Edwards's decision to move to Stockbridge came as a surprise to many people. In fact, the man in charge of the mission didn't like the idea. He thought Edwards was not sociable enough to be a good teacher and was too old to learn the languages of the natives. Also, his writings were too hard to understand. In spite of this, in April 1751 Edwards was formally installed as pastor in Stockbridge. His family joined him in October.

TIMOTHY VALENTINE

The Housatonic River by Stockbridge

It was true that Edwards was not the most sociable person. Some people said he looked distant. At the same time, he really cared for others. This became especially clear at Stockbridge, where he stood by the natives when some of the British, including his cousins, mistreated them—trading without paying a just price or paying with rum to make them drunk.

Edwards preached through an interpreter—mostly a man named John Wauwaumpequunnaunt, who knew well both the English language and the Bible. The story of the life, death, and resurrection of Jesus as the only way of salvation was still fairly new to most of the natives, so Edwards explained it in a way they could relate to, using images from nature that were familiar to them. For example, he said that "God's goodness is like a river that overflows all its bounds" and that the Word of God "is ten thousand times better than the light of the sun."

A prayer written in the Mohican language by Jonathan Edwards Jr. at age twenty

JONATHAN EDWARDS COLLECTION. GENERAL COLLECTION, BEINECKE RARE BOOK AND MANUSCRIPT LIBRARY

PHOTO BY DANNY MACHALINI

A pair of skates built in the nineteenth century and displayed
in the Village Historique Acadien. They are probably
similar to those used in Edwards's time.

The Edwards children became good friends with the natives. In the winter, they skated together on the river and sledded down the hills. "They like the place far better than they expected," Edwards wrote about them. "Here, at present, we live in peace, which has of long time been an unusual thing with us. The Indians seem much pleased with my family, especially my wife."

Edwards was also very involved in the local school. He encouraged children "to speak freely and to ask questions." He also insisted that the school include boys and girls, both English and Native Americans. This was different from most schools at that time. Sadly, some of the directors of the school didn't agree with him. Also, a fire destroyed the school building, and it took a long time to rebuild it. The Mohawks who lived in the area were interested in enrolling their children in the school but became discouraged by these problems and left.

The Edwards children skated with the natives on the river and sledded down the hills.

Edwards was disappointed. He had wanted to open his school to the Mohawks and other tribes so they could hear the message of the gospel. Finally, in the spring of 1755, the schoolmaster, Gideon Hawley, who also was licensed to preach, decided the only way to reach other natives was to go to their villages. He asked Edwards's permission to take his son Jonathan Jr., who was ten at that time, on a mission to Onohquaga, New York.

Young Jonathan had learned the Mohican and Mohawk languages from the local children and knew them so well that his thoughts ran in those languages most of the time. "I knew the names of some things in Indian which I didn't know in English," he wrote later. Edwards agreed without any hesitation, and he and Sarah escorted the missionary group as far as the paved road took them, then sent their son off into the woods with some supplies and a prayer. Jonathan Jr. returned home safely the following year.

Edwards sent his son Jonathan Jr. on a mission to the natives in Onohquaga, New York.

Hendrick Theyanoguin, a Mohawk chief who fought on the side of the British against the French. He expressed disappointment in those who opposed Edwards's plans at the Stockbridge school.

In the meantime, the war between the French, the natives, and the British raged fiercer than ever. Even though the Mohicans at Stockbridge remained neutral, the town was constantly in danger of being attacked and had to become an armed camp. The Edwardses fortified their home. They may have been tempted to leave, but, remembering Brainerd's example of self-sacrifice, they decided to stay. By that time Sarah, Esther, and Mary were married and had moved to other cities. The Edwardses sent some of the other children to live in Northampton with Mary, where they could be safer. To a friend in Scotland Edwards explained, "A dark cloud seems to hang over us. We need the prayers of all our friends."

In spite of these dangers, Edwards found time to write what have become some of his most important books, including one about original sin and another on free will. He had some good friends who shared his love for God's Word and visited him frequently for a few days at a time to read and comment on the books and essays each one was writing.

Edwards and his friends often read and commented on their writings together.

Writing these books was important to them. Many people at that time were challenging authority of every kind—the authority of kings, of the church, and even of God. There was much talk about freedom and virtue, often without mention of God's grace. Edwards wanted to help people understand that without God there can be no real freedom and no real virtue because men and women are always influenced by their sinful nature. According to the Bible, God is in control of everything, and everything happens for His glory—and that's good news because He is also perfectly loving, and His glory means our happiness.

Edwards was also planning to write a book about the great story of God's salvation of sinners from before the creation of the world till the time when all believers will be united with Jesus. He wanted to show that the Bible is really all about this story, which is still unfolding right now. He thought this book would be different from anything that had been written before.

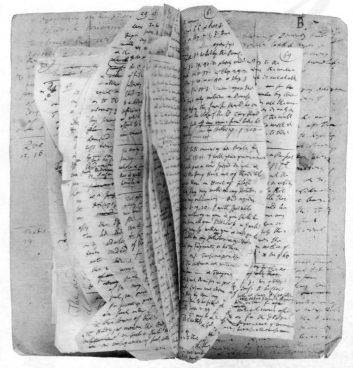

A temporary notebook made by Edwards by sowing together some scraps of the rice paper his wife and daughters had used to make fans. We can see some spots of the watercolor used to paint the fans.

CHAPTER SIX
The Last Years

In 1757, Aaron Burr died. He was the husband of Edwards's daughter Esther and the president of the College of New Jersey, which later became Princeton University. In need of a new president, the college contacted the man they considered best for the job: Jonathan Edwards.

The invitation caught Edwards by surprise. He was honored, but at the same time he knew that he had many limitations. In his answer he explained that his health was not very strong. Besides, he was easily discouraged, and when he felt depressed, he was not pleasant to have around. He also thought his knowledge of higher math and Greek was not good enough for a president of a college. Finally, he was still trying to write two more books, and he knew that running a college would prevent him from reaching that goal.

ROBERT ENGLISH

Princeton's Maclean House, built in 1756. It served as the president's residence until 1878. Aaron Burr and Jonathan Edwards lived there.

On the other hand, Edwards didn't want to make such an important decision alone, so he invited other pastors from his area to his home to ask for their advice. When the pastors arrived, they all agreed that he should accept the invitation. Edwards broke into tears. Their agreement confirmed that God wanted him to accept this task, but it was difficult to leave the mission and to move his family once again. He probably wondered if his new position would allow him time to finish the books he considered so important for the church. The following Sunday, he preached a farewell sermon to his Stockbridge church on Hebrews 13:14: "For here have we no continuing city, but we seek one to come."

As he left alone to prepare a place for his family, he gave his wife and the other children an emotional good-bye. His daughter Susannah said he left "as affectionately, as if he should not come again." After he left the house, he turned around and said, "I commit you to God," reminding himself and them that they were in God's hands.

With tears, Edwards accepted the invitation.

Soon after Edwards arrived in Princeton, however, he became enthusiastic about his calling as college president. He must also have been eager to move into the beautiful president's home with Esther Edwards Burr; her two children, Sally and Aaron Jr.; and his daughter Lucy who had moved there the spring before. There were other benefits at Princeton—especially protection from the war and a library of over twelve hundred books. As president of the college, he also had the chance to prepare students to serve God in their different duties and to face the unbiblical teachings he had been fighting in his books. Initially, however, he just tried to get used to the place while preaching to the college staff and students every Sunday. Sarah and his other children were scheduled to join him after the winter.

He had, however, a serious concern. Smallpox, a deadly illness, was spreading around the region. Lucy had already caught it and survived, but Edwards didn't want anyone else in his family to catch it. To prevent it, on February 23 he received an inoculation and made sure his family did the same.

Esther Edwards Burr
YALE UNIVERSITY ART GALLERY,
BEQUEST OF OLIVER BURR JENNINGS, B.A. 1917,
IN MEMORY OF MISS ANNIE BURR JENNINGS

Inoculation was a method of prevention that had been used in countries like Africa, India, and China for centuries. It was different from today's vaccination because it was done by injecting a little portion of the live virus into someone's arm. Today, most of the vaccines don't contain the active disease.

Normally, the inoculation gave people a small case of the disease, which forced them to produce enough antibodies to fight any stronger attacks. As expected, Edwards had a small case of smallpox. His body, however, was too weak to fight, and the fever became worse. Soon he realized he was dying, so he called Lucy to his side and asked her to write down one last message to his wife and children. To his wife, he said their marriage had been an "uncommon [very special] union" that would "continue forever."

After that, he could hardly speak, and everyone thought he was unconscious. To their surprise, he found enough strength to say, "Trust in God, and ye need not fear." Those were his last words. He died on March 22, 1758.

His death was followed by other sad events. Two weeks later, his daughter Esther died of a fever. It was not smallpox, but the inoculation might have weakened her body. His wife, Sarah, was ill with a different sickness when she received the news of their deaths, and she could not travel for a few months. In September she went to the college to pick up her grandchildren but became ill again and died in Philadelphia on October 2, 1758. One of the Edwards daughters, Elizabeth, died of another illness a few months later.

DR. OLIVER CRISP

Since Jonathan Edwards worked many hours and gave little attention to food, he was very thin. This painting by Dr. Oliver Crisp is probably more true to reality than the best known portrait.

Jonathan Edwards continues to have a great influence on his readers. Today, there are twenty-six volumes of his works in print, and some of his writings are still being discovered and transcribed. Even people who disagree with his ideas find his works original and interesting because they make readers think about important subjects.

Edwards is mostly remembered for his role in the First Great Awakening, an event in which many people were converted. During that exciting but often confusing time, he called all to repentance and faith in Christ and reminded them to follow the Bible instead of unbiblical emotions and to respect the church and its leaders.

He also spent a great deal of time considering some of the big questions that were coming up in his day, as the birth of democracies and the dawn of a new method of science brought new ideas about freedom and justice. He often answered with more questions such as, What do we mean by words like *freedom* and *virtue*? Can a sinful person really be free? He wanted to help people understand that we can't try to match the Bible to our own ideas. We have to discover God as He has revealed Himself in the Scriptures, as He is so immense, amazing, and perfect that no one can ever judge Him by human standards.

Time Line of Jonathan Edwards's Life

1703–Edwards is born on October 5 at East Windsor, Connecticut.

1716–He is admitted to Yale University.

1720–He graduates from Yale and continues to study to become a pastor.

1722–He serves as pastor of a New York church for eight months.

1724–He is elected a tutor at Yale.

1726–He serves as assistant minister to Solomon Stoddard, his grandfather.

1727–He marries Sarah Pierpont on July 28.

1729–He becomes senior pastor upon the death of Solomon Stoddard.

1734–A revival starts in Northampton—the first part of what became known as the First Great Awakening.

1737–Edwards's *A Faithful Narrative of the Surprising Work of God* becomes a guide and inspiration for the Great Awakening.

1740–George Whitefield visits New England. God uses his visits to the colonies to usher in the second and most widespread part of the First Great Awakening.

1741–Edwards preaches "Sinners in the Hands of an Angry God" in Enfield, Connecticut.

1744–The First Great Awakening diminishes in New England.

1746–Edwards writes *A Treatise on Religious Affections*.

1747–David Brainerd dies at the Edwards home. Seventeen-year-old Jerusha Edwards dies four months later.

1750–Edwards is dismissed as pastor of the church in Northampton.

1751–He becomes pastor and missionary to the Native Americans in Stockbridge, Massachusetts.

1758–He is inaugurated president of Princeton College on February 16, then dies on March 22 after a smallpox inoculation.

Did you know?

❧ Everyone in Edwards's family was tall. His ten sisters were so tall that people used to say jokingly that Timothy Edwards had sixty feet of daughters.

❧ Unlike most women in those days, all of Jonathan's sisters received a thorough education. One of them, Esther, wrote an essay to answer people who thought human souls were material. It was written so well that for many years people thought Jonathan was the author.

❧ Timothy Edwards pastored the same church for fifty-six years, which was not unusual in those days. Pastors often stayed in the same church until they died. Also, people didn't move from church to church as they sometimes do today. They just went to the church in the place where they lived.

❧ Esther Stoddard Edwards, Jonathan's mother, was well known for her kindness, wisdom, and knowledge of the Scriptures. She continued to hold Bible studies for women in her house until she was in her nineties. She lived a long life and died twelve years after Jonathan's death.

❧ When Jonathan was young, most toys were homemade. Some popular toys were balls, kites, marbles, jump ropes, and hoops and sticks. Girls often played with dolls made out of cornhusks.

❧ In college, Edwards kept a notebook with scientific questions he wanted to answer: Why is air necessary to preserve a fire? Why are no two trees exactly alike? What makes a bubble break? Why is the heat of the sun's rays greater near the surface of the earth than higher up? Why do waves form as they do? Why does lightning not travel in a straight line, and why do repeated flashes follow the same pattern? Why is the sky blue? Why is the sun not perfectly white?

❧ Benjamin Franklin, the famous inventor and one of the Founding Fathers of the United States, went to hear George Whitefield preach. He later wrote that the preacher had a "loud and clear voice." To see how many people could hear the sermon, he walked through the streets of Philadelphia while Whitefield was speaking until the sound of his voice faded. By this experiment, he estimated that thirty thousand people could hear the message.

❧ People in Edwards's day wrote with quill and ink. The quill was usually a goose feather, but some people used feathers from turkeys and swans. Crow feathers produced the best quills. The feathers were collected at molting time when they naturally fell off the birds. Then they were cleansed in boiling water and cut at an angle with a pen knife. After the pit was removed, another cut was made around the middle of the feather to provide an even flow of ink. When the tip of the quill became dull or cracked, the writer had to repeat the process until the quill became too short to be used. When quills were not in use, they had to be kept damp, usually in a quill holder or glass cup.

❧ Even ink was often homemade from different ingredients: gum arabic, ferrous sulfate, oak galls, and rainwater or white wine. First, the oak galls were crushed, mixed with the water or wine, placed in the sun for a day or two, and then strained. Then the ferrous sulfate was added, and the mixture was left in the sun for another day or two. Gum arabic was the last ingredient. To make the ink glossy, it was simmered over the fire with some sugar. The ink was kept in bottles. When people traveled, they often kept ink inside the horn of an ox or cow that was closed by a lid on the wide end.

❧ People had to buy paper, but it wasn't as easy to get then as it is today. When people went to Boston, Edwards often asked them to buy some paper for him. Since it was expensive, he used scraps of paper for his notes. Sometimes he wrote on margins of old sermons or even of newspapers. He usually made his own notebooks and used the brown wrapper that held the paper reams together to make a cover. Once he used a piece of wallpaper. Finally, he wrote the title of each book on the front, on the back, and on the side, in two directions, so he could always see what it was, no matter how he laid the book on the table.

❧ To keep some of his books at hand, Edwards commissioned a lazy Susan book table with a rotating top. It was probably his invention.

❧ Edwards loved music and made sure it was taught in the schools he supervised. His family owned a few instruments and sang psalms and hymns every day during family devotions.

❧ Chocolate was a favorite item in the Edwards home, usually served as a beverage for breakfast. It was still rare in those days, but Edwards bought some whenever he traveled to Boston or some other large city. Other luxury items the people in Northampton imported from Boston were sugar, raisins, and ribbons.

❧ Once when Esther Burr Edwards was sick, Edwards wrote her a letter, adding some practical suggestions for her health. He told her to try a root called ginseng stewed in water or wine. His wife suggested another herb called Robin's plantain or some type of spread made of raisins for her strength. Edwards also suggested a remedy that had helped Esther before: a rattlesnake! In fact, he said he had found one for her and was going to send it.

* In many churches during Edwards's time, decisions were made by official meetings of ministers and elders. When it came to important teachings, they all followed the historical Protestant documents called confessions. But Edwards's church in Northampton was a type of church called Congregational because the congregation of members had the final say in decisions. Also, pastors had the freedom to disagree with the usual practice or teachings of the local church. This is why Edwards could disagree with the way the Lord's Supper was served and why the congregation had the right to expel him.

* When the Europeans arrived to settle in America, the continent was home to many native peoples, nations, and cultures, each with its own history. Most of them survived by hunting, fishing, and growing food—especially corn, beans, and squash.

* The name *Mohican* (also spelled Mahican) was originally Muh-he-cun-nuk, which means "people who follow the flowing rivers." The Mohicans were mostly seasonal hunters.

* Gideon Hawley, the schoolmaster who traveled with Jonathan Edwards Jr. to bring the gospel to the Mohawks, finally left Stockbridge to live with the Mashpee tribe on Cape Cod, Massachusetts, and stayed there for nearly fifty years, until his death.

* One of the Stockbridge Mohicans, Hendrick Aupaumut, who was probably baptized by Edwards, translated some of Edwards's works and the Westminster Shorter Catechism into the Mohican language.

A Letter from Edwards to His Daughter Mary

July 26, 1749
Northampton, Massachusetts

Dear Child,

　You may well think that it is natural for a parent to be concerned for a child at so great a distance, so far out of view, and so far out of the reach of communication where, if you should be taken with any dangerous sickness that should issue in death, you might probably be in your grave before we could hear of your danger.

　But yet my greatest concern is for your soul's good. Though you are at so great a distance from us, yet God is everywhere. You are much out of the reach of our care, but you are every moment in His hands. We have not the comfort of seeing you, but He sees you—His eye is always upon you. And if you may but be sensibly nigh to Him and have His gracious presence, it is no matter though you are far distant from us. I had rather you should remain hundreds of miles distant from us and have God nigh to you by His Spirit than to have you always with us and live at a distance from God. And if the next news we should hear of you should be of your death (though that would be very sad), yet if we should hear of that which should give great grounds to hope that you had died in the Lord, how much more comfortable would this be than if we should be with you in all your sickness and have much opportunity to tend you and converse and pray with you and take an affectionate leave of you and after all have reason to learn that you died without God's grace and favor!

It is comfortable to have the presence of earthly friends, especially in sickness and on a deathbed, but the great thing is to have God as our friend and to be united to Christ, who can never die anymore and from whom our death can't separate us. My desire and daily prayer is that you may, if it may consist with the holy will of God, meet with God where you are and have much of His divine influences on your heart wherever you may be, and that in God's due time you may be returned to us again in all respects under the smiles of heaven, and especially in prosperous circumstances in your soul and that you may find us alive. But that is uncertain; for you know what a dying time it has been with us in this town about this time of year in years past. May God fit us all for His will.

I hope you will maintain a strict and constant watch over yourself and against all temptations—that you don't forget and forsake God and particularly that you don't grow slack in secret religion. Retire often from this vain world and all its bubbles, empty shadows, and vain amusements and converse with God alone. And seek that divine grace and comfort, the least drop of which is more worth than all the riches, gaiety, pleasures, and entertainments of the whole world.

We are all by God's goodness in a fair state of health. The whole family has indeed much to make us sensible of our dependence on God's care and kindness and of the vanity of all human dependence, and we are very loudly called to seek His face, trust in Him, and walk closely with Him. Commending to the care and special favor of a heavenly Father, I am

Your very affectionate father,
Jonathan Edwards

Your mother and all the family give their love to you.

Acknowledgments

Once again, I have many people to thank for the making of this book, particularly Dr. Kenneth P. Minkema, executive director of the Jonathan Edwards Center and Online Archive at Yale University, and Dr. Oliver D. Crisp, professor of systematic theology at Fuller Theological Seminary in Pasadena, California, and author of *Jonathan Edwards and the Metaphysics of Sin*, who read the manuscript and very patiently answered my frequent questions. Other people who agreed to read my manuscript and provided important feedback include Dr. Darryl G. Hart, professor of history at Hillsdale College in Hillsdale, Michigan; Timothy Massaro, graduate of Westminster Seminary, California; and my friend Heather Chisholm-Chait. Dr. Ralph Mason, professor of education at the University of Manitoba and author of several articles on Isaac Newton, has also kindly provided some needed assistance in understanding the scientific environment of Edwards's day.

I have also had the privilege of reading the book to an insightful and lively audience—my Sunday school class of fourth through sixth graders: Isaiah Brindis De Salas; Nathan and Alison Thumann; Zoe and Evan Olow; and James, Matthew, Olivia, and Adam Horton. Their comments have been encouraging and invaluable.

As always, I am very grateful to everyone who has provided photos free of charge or for a minimal fee as well as to Tom Carroll, my map illustrator, and Matt Abraxas, the main illustrator for this series. This book could not be what it is without their generous help.

Finally, I am deeply grateful for the support I have received from my husband, Tom, and my children; from my church family at Christ United Reformed Church; and from the staff at Reformation Heritage Books, who went far beyond their call of duty to provide all the assistance I needed.